The Urbana Free Library

To renew: call 217-367-4057
or go to *"urbanafreelibrary.org"*
and select "Renew/Request Items"

Wild Stunts

MIND-BLOWING
MOVIE
STUNTS

by Joe Tougas

CAPSTONE PRESS
a capstone imprint

Edge Books are published by Capstone Press,
1710 Roe Crest Drive, North Mankato, Minnesota 56003
www.capstonepub.com

Library of Congress Cataloging-in-Publication Data
Tougas, Joe
 Mind-blowing movie stunts / by Joe Tougas.
   pages cm.—(Edge books. wild stunts.)
 Summary: "Describes movie stunts, including who accomplished these stunts and,
to a certain degree, how"—Provided by publisher.
 Includes bibliographical references and index.
 ISBN 978-1-4914-4256-2 (library binding)
 ISBN 978-1-4914-4317-0 (eBook PDF)
1. Stunt performers—Juvenile literature. I. Title.
 PN1995.9.S7T68 2016
 791.402'8—dc23
                          2015002861

Editorial Credits
Nate LeBoutillier, editor; Kyle Grenz, designer; Jo Miller, media researcher;
Tori Abraham, production specialist

Photo Credits
Alamy: AF archive, 15, 28-29, Moviestore collection Ltd, 6-7, Ronald Grant Archive,
9; Corbis: Bettmann, 19; Getty Images: Historic Photo Archive, 10; Newscom: akg-
images, 5, Album/M.G.M., 25, Album/UNIVERSAL PICTURES, 26-27, Beltia
Archives Digital Press Photos, 8, picture-alliance, cover, 11, 12-13, ZUMA Press/
Alpha, 21, ZUMA Press/Bryan Smith, 20; The Kobal Collection: DANJAQ/EON/UA,
17, GOLDEN HARVEST COMPANY, 23, UNIVERSAL, 24

Design Elements
Shutterstock: antishock, Igorsky, Leigh Prather, NEGOVURA, Radoman Durkovic

Direct Quotations
Pages 18 and 22 from 2011 book *The True Adventures of the World's Greatest
Stuntman: My Life as Indiana Jones, James Bond, Superman and Other Movie Heroes*
by Vic Armstrong, published by Titan Books

Printed in the United States of America in North Mankato, Minnesota.
032015   008823CGF15

Table of Contents

Hearts Pounding, Eyes Widening, Minds Blown

When we decide to watch a movie, the last thing we want is to see something ordinary. We watch scary movies to get chills. We watch love stories to make us feel good. We watch *comedies* to make us laugh and feel silly. And we watch action movies because they can get our hearts pounding, our eyes widening, and our minds blown.

Good action movies make us ask two important questions: "How did they DO that?" and "What on Earth will they do next?" Movies have come a long way since the early days of silent black-and-white films to the multi-million dollar movies of today. As time passes, moviemakers create films that are more action-packed, more death-defying, and more amazing than the year before. Let's look at some incredible stunts, the people who make them, and where it's all heading.

comedy—a funny play or film

On November 10, 1921, an uncredited actor only identified as "Fearless Freddie" jumps from a plane in one of the first filmed stunts.

Early and Dangerous Days of Amazing Movie Stunts

Excitement from the Start

Motion pictures—also called movies—were first shown to *audiences* around 1895. By the early 1900s, movies were a very popular form of entertainment. People were amazed to see movement on a flat screen. It didn't matter if that movement was somebody simply walking down the street or riding a horse.

The Keystone Cops act for an early film scene.

audience—people who watch or listen to a play, movie, or show

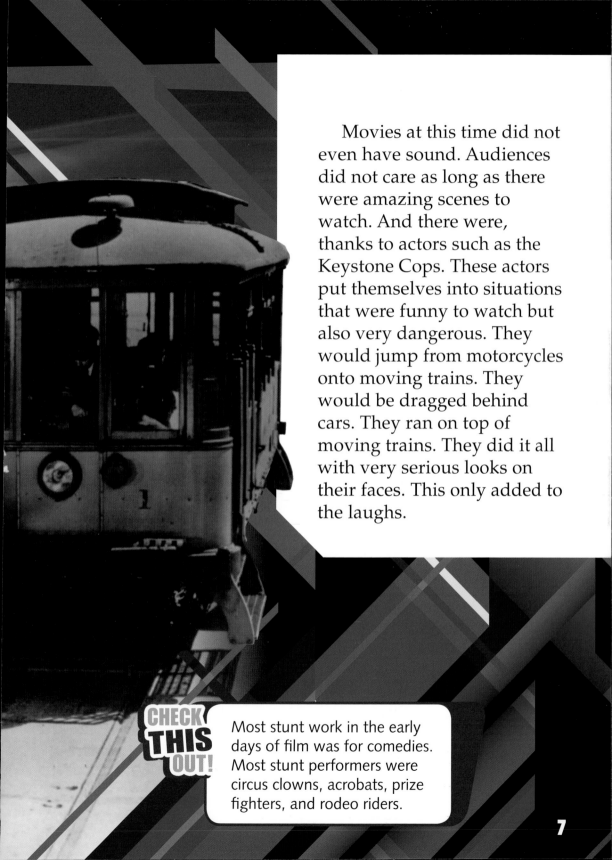

Movies at this time did not even have sound. Audiences did not care as long as there were amazing scenes to watch. And there were, thanks to actors such as the Keystone Cops. These actors put themselves into situations that were funny to watch but also very dangerous. They would jump from motorcycles onto moving trains. They would be dragged behind cars. They ran on top of moving trains. They did it all with very serious looks on their faces. This only added to the laughs.

CHECK THIS OUT!

Most stunt work in the early days of film was for comedies. Most stunt performers were circus clowns, acrobats, prize fighters, and rodeo riders.

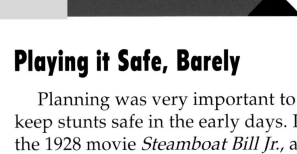

Playing it Safe, Barely

Planning was very important to keep stunts safe in the early days. In the 1928 movie *Steamboat Bill Jr.*, an entire front of a house falls down with actor Buster Keaton standing in harm's way. But Keaton knew exactly where to stand so that the house fell around him. His spot was under an open window. One tiny mistake in his **calculations** could have been deadly.

Buster Keaton checks a cannon in the 1926 film *The General*.

CHECK THIS OUT!

In the film world, stunts are called "gags."

Buster Keaton pulls off the famous house stunt in *Steamboat Bill Jr.*

Like the Keystone Cops, Keaton's stunts were funny but risky. During a stunt in the 1924 film *Sherlock Jr.*, a powerful stream of water rushes down on his head. For this small bit of comedy, Keaton nearly broke his neck.

Most movie stars were not interested in risking injury. This gave rise to a new job in films, that of the ***stunt double***. Stunt doubles were also known as stuntmen or stuntwomen.

calculation—use of a mathematical process to determine an outcome

stunt double—a person who takes the place of an actress or actor in an action scene or when a special skill or great risk is called for

The Rise of the Stunt Double

Filmmakers used stunt doubles to take the place of the main characters. The stunt doubles stood in only for a few seconds, when action was at its riskiest. One of the most famous stunt doubles of all time was a former rodeo champion named Yakima Canutt.

Canutt performed what many say is the greatest stunt ever filmed. It was in the 1939 film series *Zorro's Fighting Legion*. In the stunt Canutt rides a galloping horse alongside a team of horses pulling a wagon. He jumps off his horse and onto the hitch that connects the team. The horse team continues speeding along as Canutt falls underneath the hitch but hangs on. From there he moves himself under the galloping horses to the back of the wagon. Climbing back on, he overtakes the bad guys he's been chasing.

Yakima Canutt

One of the most famous stunts of all time was performed by Harold Lloyd. In the 1923 movie *Safety Last!*, Lloyd hangs on to the arm of a large outdoor clock. His body dangles far above ground. Though it seems that Lloyd is in danger of falling 13 stories, in reality he was only in danger of falling a short distance.

Viewers were amazed, and they wanted more. They got it. Canutt did the same stunt in two other films. By then moviegoers had a growing appetite for action. Movie studios were happy to deliver.

More, More, More! The Rise of Action Films

The Legendary Chariot Race

Since the late 1950s, action movies have kept stunt men and women very busy. They put their lives in danger just to film a good scene.

One movie that gave audiences both a good story and a giant taste of action was *Ben-Hur*. This 1959 film was set in ancient Rome. It is remembered for its exciting *chariot* race in a Roman arena. In the race, horse-drawn chariots crash and rip apart at high speeds. Their drivers fall and tumble over and over on the dirt track. One racer, his chariot smashed, hangs onto his horses' reins while being dragged across the dusty ground. When he finally lets go, he is run over by another chariot and team of horses.

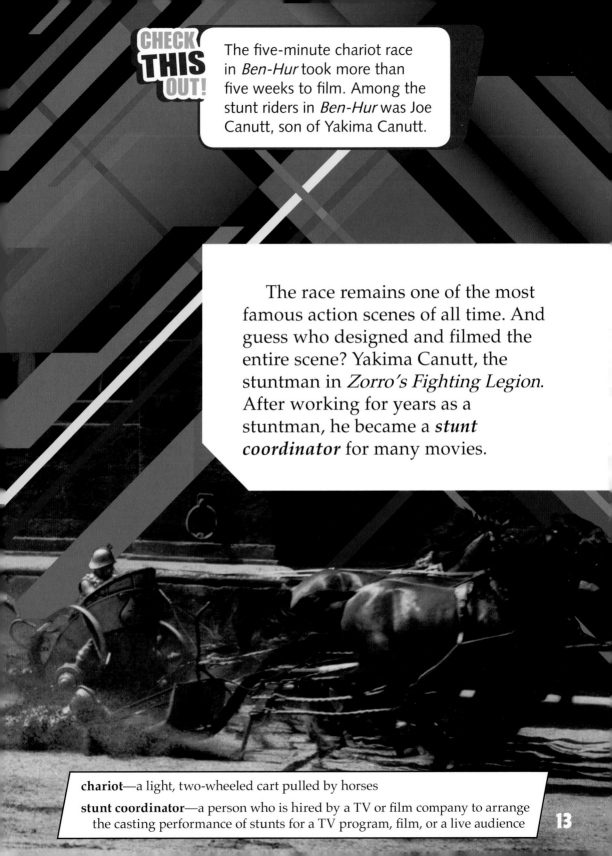

The five-minute chariot race in *Ben-Hur* took more than five weeks to film. Among the stunt riders in *Ben-Hur* was Joe Canutt, son of Yakima Canutt.

The race remains one of the most famous action scenes of all time. And guess who designed and filmed the entire scene? Yakima Canutt, the stuntman in *Zorro's Fighting Legion*. After working for years as a stuntman, he became a *stunt coordinator* for many movies.

chariot—a light, two-wheeled cart pulled by horses

stunt coordinator—a person who is hired by a TV or film company to arrange the casting performance of stunts for a TV program, film, or a live audience

When Once is Enough

Some movies are memorable for using one big stunt, but using it beautifully. In the memorable chase scene from the popular 1982 movie *E.T. the Extra-Terrestrial,* kids race and jump on BMX bikes. Angry policemen and evil scientists want to capture the young hero, Elliot, and his alien friend, E.T. Suddenly, when it seems the kids are sure to be caught, their bikes rise off the ground and fly. The scene had audiences cheering in surprise. It also led to a 1980s BMX bike boom.

Likewise, many children continue to be amazed by the 1964 movie *Mary Poppins.* In this movie, Mary Poppins is a nanny in 1910 London. She is able to travel by floating in the air and landing softly on the ground by simply using an umbrella. This stunt looks so real that many kids, even today, try to see if umbrellas actually help break a jump's fall. (They don't. The only thing that gets broken might be a leg!)

CHECK **THIS** OUT!

There were eight stunt doubles used in the *E.T.* BMX bike chase scene. Mostly teenaged boys, they were chosen from a local BMX track in Torrance, California.

As Stunts Get Better, Safety Measures Grow

Action movies became very popular in the 1960s and 1970s. And no such film was complete without at least one good chase scene. One popular film series featured secret agent James Bond. Across the world Bond chased or was chased by *villains* on cars, motorcycles, helicopters, and even skis. In one famous stunt from *The Man With The Golden Gun*, Bond drives an AMC Hornet onto a broken bridge. The car then flies over a small river pass, spinning as it soars through the air before landing on all four wheels.

In the 1960s and 70s, filmmakers and stunt coordinators began creating equipment to help improve stunts and safety. The car flip in 1974's *The Man With The Golden Gun* was the first of its kind. It used a computer to map out the jump and calculate distance. This information made the stunt safer and more controlled. While safety measures improved in the stunt world, it did not mean stunt work was completely safe.

villain—a wicked, evil, or bad person who is often a character in a story

movie director—a person who directs the making of a film and controls a film's artistic and dramatic aspects

second unit director—a person on a film set who is in charge of a small crew and is responsible for filming stunts, crowds, and scenery

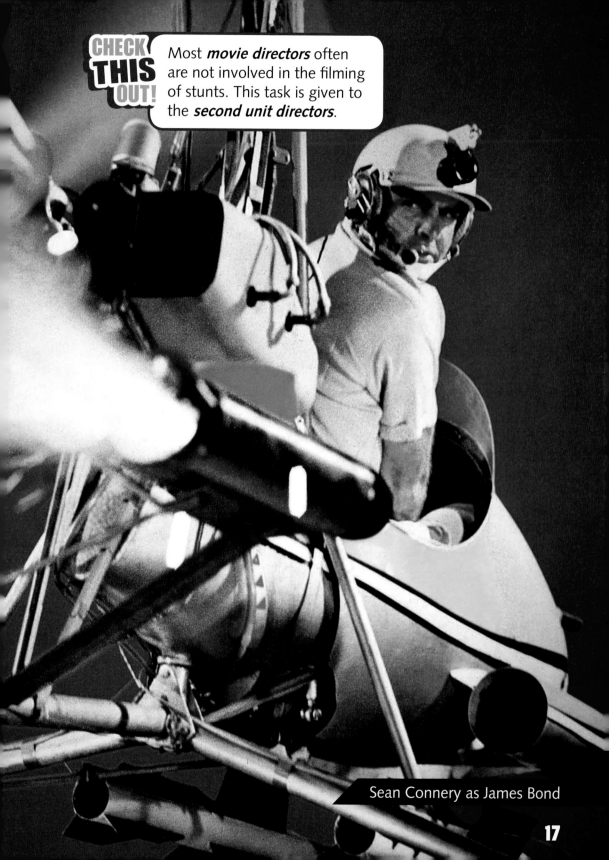

CHECK THIS OUT!

Most *movie directors* often are not involved in the filming of stunts. This task is given to the *second unit directors*.

Sean Connery as James Bond

Who Would Do This?

When Stunts Go Bad

Being a stuntman or stuntwoman is always going to be a dangerous job. Today special equipment is available for safety, but accidents can still happen. Over the years many accidents—even deaths—have happened on movie sets during stunt filming.

"Over my years as a stuntman I've broken my shin, my arm, my nose and my collarbone, busted my ribs, and knackered one heel."
stuntman Vic Armstrong

WILD BUT TRUE!

Ever wonder how cars flip over the way they do in chase scenes or big crashes? This stunt involves a piece of equipment called a "cannon," a metal jack underneath one side of a car. When activated, the jack shoots out from below the speeding car, rapidly lifting one side and causing it to overturn on its side and roll over at high speeds.

In 1982 actor Vic Morrow and two children were killed in an action scene. A helicopter crashed as they were filming an action scene in *The Twilight Zone*. In 1986 stuntman Dar Robinson, known for being very safety-minded, died performing a stunt. He was to drive a motorcycle into a guardrail at 40 miles (64 kilometers) per hour. But his cycle went off a cliff in the desert. He died from his injuries.

What makes stunts exciting also makes them often highly dangerous. While deaths are rare, injuries are common among stunt doubles. Thousands have been injured on the job.

Scene of the tragic helicopter accident during filming of the 1982 movie *The Twilight Zone*.

It's What They Love To Do

So why would somebody want to risk injury or even death for a living? Many stunt performers see it as a way to keep doing what they love. Vic Armstrong loved riding and racing horses. He was asked in 1966 to supply a good running horse and rider (himself) for the movie *Arabesque*. As he helped on the film, he saw it as a good way to make money doing what he enjoyed. He went on to a 40-year career in stunt work.

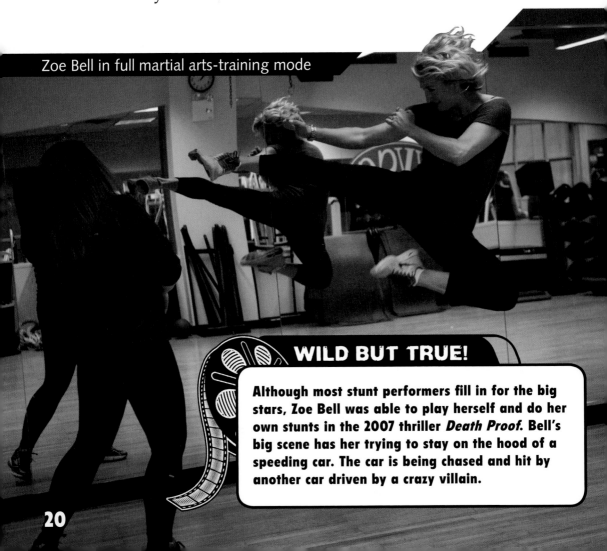

Zoe Bell in full martial arts-training mode

WILD BUT TRUE!

Although most stunt performers fill in for the big stars, Zoe Bell was able to play herself and do her own stunts in the 2007 thriller *Death Proof*. Bell's big scene has her trying to stay on the hood of a speeding car. The car is being chased and hit by another car driven by a crazy villain.

Stuntwoman Zoe Bell of New Zealand saw stunt work as a way to get paid for doing *gymnastics* and *martial arts*. At age 15, Bell was on New Zealand's national gymnastics squad. She met a stunt worker at the gymnasium. That led to her career as a stunt double that included work for Lucy Lawless in the television show *Xena: Warrior Princess*.

Lucy Lawless as
Xena the Warrior Princess

gymnastics—physical exercises, often performed on special equipment, that involve difficult and carefully controlled body movements

martial arts—styles of self-defense and fighting; tae kwon do, judo, and karate are examples of martial arts

All of the Danger, None of the Fame

Stunt performers certainly don't do what they do for fame. Most stunt performers know that they will not become famous like the stars they replace on screen. The movie studios prefer it this way to keep the feeling that it's just one person performing, not two.

Armstrong says he doesn't mind. "People say to me, 'Don't you get bitter when you see the stars getting [attention] for all the stunts you've done?' and I always say, 'Absolutely not.' I couldn't act to save my life ... The audience goes to see their heroes the stars, not the stunt man."

WILD BUT TRUE!

The only time the *Academy Awards* recognized stunt performers at all was in 1966. Yakima Canutt was given an award for his work and for the safety equipment he made to help protect stunt performers. Many in the film industry continue to push for more recognition for stuntmen and stuntwomen from The Academy.

Academy Awards—an annual American awards ceremony honoring film achievements

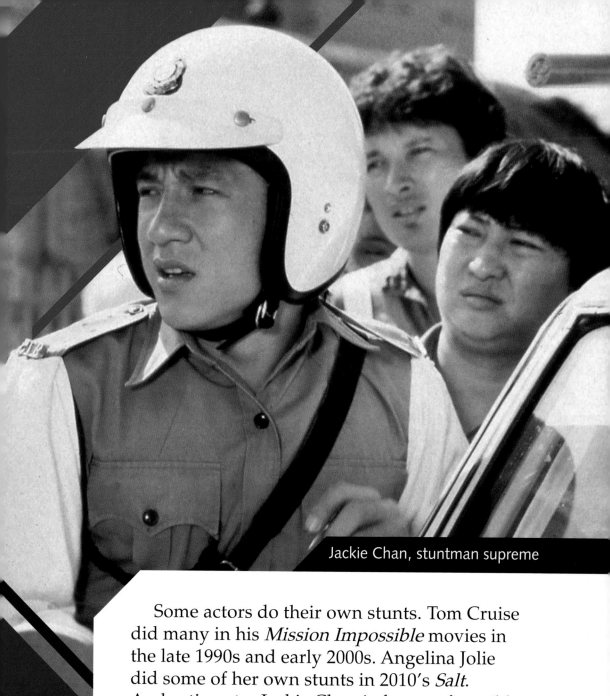

Jackie Chan, stuntman supreme

Some actors do their own stunts. Tom Cruise did many in his *Mission Impossible* movies in the late 1990s and early 2000s. Angelina Jolie did some of her own stunts in 2010's *Salt*. And action star Jackie Chan is famous for wild stunts he creates. That's him hanging from a flying helicopter's rope ladder in 1992's *Super Cop*. And that's him making audiences gasp as he roller skates under speeding semi trucks in 1983's *Winners and Sinners*.

Saving the Day: Stunt Animals

Some of the most hard-working stunt performers are animals. The 1995 movie *Babe* is about a pig that lives on a farm with dogs and learns to herd sheep. The stunt here is not so much jumping or falling, but acting. Thanks to good direction of a great story, audiences of all ages enjoyed *Babe*. They enjoyed believing that Babe and the other animals in the movie actually talked to each other.

CHECK THIS OUT!

An attractive show dog was chosen for the role of Lassie in 1943's *Lassie Come Home*. But when the fancy collie wouldn't jump in water, a stunt dog named Pal was called in. Even though Pal was male (it was assumed Lassie was a female) and not a purebred collie, his stunt work won him the starring role. The show dog was fired. Pal went on to star in six more movies.

The most famous animal in movies and TV is Lassie. This collie was always smart enough to rescue its owner from danger or point out bad guys before they got away. Lassie was the star of a popular television show in the 1950s. Several Lassie movies have been made over the years, from *Lassie Come Home* in 1943 to *Lassie* in 2005.

The Future of Movie Stunts

What's in Store for Stunts?

In recent years, more and more films are using computers to create dangerous scenes. This is known as *computer-generated imagery* (CGI). Today it is not unusual at all to see sweeping ocean waves cover an entire city or a giant monster such as Godzilla knocking over the buildings of downtown San Francisco.

CHECK THIS OUT!

The 1973 science fiction film *Westworld* is considered the first to use CGI. When the movie showed how a killer robot saw things, it was all in small squares, or *pixels*, much like how the game Minecraft looks.

computer-generated imagery (CGI)—animated graphics produced by a computer and used in film or TV

pixel—one of the tiny dots on a video screen or computer monitor that make up a visual image

Indeed, computers today can make things appear on film that would have been impossible years ago. In fact, many movies wouldn't have been made if not for CGI. The 2005 re-make of *King Kong* is one. The giant ape fights and defeats two killer dinosaurs in one of many CGI scenes. The exciting pod race in 1999's *Star Wars: Episode I – The Phantom Menace* was produced entirely with CGI. This poses an interesting question: Is it the end of the stuntman and stuntwoman, if computers can take the risks for them? In two words: No way.

Real Stunts Are Here to Stay

That's still a real person jumping out of an airplane in 2013's *Iron Man 3*. And that's stuntwoman Heidi Moneymaker kicking, swooping, and knocking out bad guys—all while tied to a chair—in 2012's *The Avengers*. Like the audiences in the early 1900s, we are still able to be amazed. And it's most often by watching real people perform real stunt work. We may enjoy the way CGI looks, but we like how real stunts make us feel.

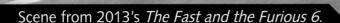

Scene from 2013's *The Fast and the Furious 6*.

CHECK THIS OUT!

CGI has come to a point where it can help actors appear to be older or younger better than makeup. In 2010's *Tron: Legacy*, actor Jeff Bridges, who was 61, was able to appear as he looked in the original *Tron*, which came out in 1982.

Good action movies today such as *The Fast and the Furious* films will combine both stunt performers and computer effects. This gives us both interesting scenes as well as the thrills of seeing great human stunts. We want to know if they'll be okay. We want to know how they're going to get out of a jam. And we want to know what they plan to do next to make us go, *Wow!*

Glossary

Academy Awards (uh-KAD-uh-mee uh-WARDZ)—an annual American awards ceremony honoring film achievements

audience (AW-dee-uhns)—people who watch or listen to a play, movie, or show

calculation (kal-kyuh-LAY-shuhn)—use of a mathematical process to determine an outcome

chariot (CHAYR-ee-uht)—a light, two-wheeled cart pulled by horses

comedy (KOM-uh-dee)—a funny play or film

computer-generated imagery (CGI) (kuhm-PYOO-tuhr-jen-uh-rey-ted IM-ij-ree)—animated graphics produced by a computer and used in film or TV

gymnastics (jim-NASS-tiks)—physical exercises, often performed on special equipment, that involve difficult and carefully controlled body movements

martial arts (MAR-shuhl ARTS)—styles of self-defense and fighting; tae kwon do, judo, and karate are examples of martial arts

movie director (MOO-vee duh-REK-tuhr)—a person who directs the making of a film and controls a film's artistic and dramatic aspects

pixel (PIKS-uhl)—one of the tiny dots on a video screen or computer monitor that make up a visual image

second unit director (SEK-uhnd YOO-nit duh-REK-tuhr)—a person on a film set who is in charge of a small crew and is responsible for filming stunts, crowds, and scenery

stunt coordinator (STUHNT koh-OR-duh-nay-tuhr)—a person who is hired by a TV or film company to arrange the casting performance of stunts for a TV program, film, or a live audience

stunt double (STUHNT DUH-buhl)—a person who takes the place of an actress or actor in an action scene or when a special skill or great risk is called for

villain (VIL-uhn)—a wicked, evil, or bad person who is often a character in a story

Read More

Hammelef, Danielle S. *Explosive Scenes: Fireballs, Furious Storms, and More Live Special Effects.* Awesome Special Effects. North Mankato, Minn.: Blazers Books, 2015.

Thomas, Isabel. *Being a Stunt Performer.* On The Radar: Awesome Jobs. Minneapolis, Minn.: Lerner Publications Co., 2013.

Wood, Alix. *Stunt Performer.* The World's Coolest Jobs. New York: PowerKids Press, 2014.

Internet Sites

FactHound offers a safe, fun way to find Internet sites related to this book. All of the sites on FactHound have been researched by our staff.

Here's all you do:

Visit *www.facthound.com*

Type in this code: 9781491442562

 Check out projects, games and lots more at **www.capstonekids.com**

Index